THE POETRY OF EUROPIUM

The Poetry of Europium

Walter the Educator

Silent King Books a WhichHead Imprint

Copyright © 2024 by Walter the Educator

All rights reserved. No part of this book may be reproduced in any manner whatsoever without written permission except in the case of brief quotations embodied in critical articles and reviews.

First Printing, 2024

Disclaimer
This book is a literary work; poems are not about specific persons, locations, situations, and/or circumstances unless mentioned in a historical context. This book is for entertainment and informational purposes only. The author and publisher offer this information without warranties expressed or implied. No matter the grounds, neither the author nor the publisher will be accountable for any losses, injuries, or other damages caused by the reader's use of this book. The use of this book acknowledges an understanding and acceptance of this disclaimer.

"Earning a degree in chemistry changed my life!"
– Walter the Educator

dedicated to all the chemistry lovers, like myself, across the world

CONTENTS

Dedication v

Why I Created This Book? 1
One - Symbol Of Hope 2
Two - Europium, The Cosmic Poet 4
Three - Shining Bright 6
Four - Your Radiance 8
Five - Unity And Grace 10
Six - Wonders Of The Night 12
Seven - Science Defines 14
Eight - Magic That Chemistry Derives . . . 16
Nine - Europium, A Marvel 18
Ten - Harmony And Grace 20
Eleven - Wonders Of Creation 22
Twelve - Dazzling Element 24

Thirteen - Science Unfold 26

Fourteen - Beacon Of Curiosity 28

Fifteen - Earth's Embrace 30

Sixteen - Never Ends 32

Seventeen - Day By Day 34

Eighteen - Celestial Gem 36

Nineteen - Tapestry Of Atoms 38

Twenty - Sparks The Soul 40

Twenty-One - Enlightens The Soul 42

Twenty-Two - Priceless Pearl 44

Twenty-Three - Bridging The Gaps 46

Twenty-Four - Element Of Fascination 48

Twenty-Five - Electron's Journey 50

Twenty-Six - Unique Role 52

Twenty-Seven - Catalyst Of Discovery 54

Twenty-Eight - Wisdom And Insight 56

Twenty-Nine - Periodic Scheme 58

Thirty - Europium, A Jewel 60

Thirty-One - Europium So Rare 62

Thirty-Two - Spark The Flame 64

Thirty-Three - Expanse Of Science 66

Thirty-Four - Universe's Decree 68

Thirty-Five - Forever Cherished 70

About The Author 72

WHY I CREATED THIS BOOK?

Creating a poetry book about Europium provides a unique opportunity to blend science and art, explore uncharted territories, and offer readers a fresh perspective on the world. It allows me to tap into the beauty and intrigue of this chemical element, creating a captivating and thought-provoking collection of poems.

ONE

SYMBOL OF HOPE

Europium, the element of wonder,
A luminescent jewel, shining yonder.
With atomic number sixty-three,
In the periodic table, you reside, so free.

A rare earth metal, precious and pure,
In your essence, brilliance does endure.
Discovered in eighteen eighty-six,
By Eugène-Anatole Demarçay's clever tricks.

Your name derived from the continent,
Europe's honor, you represent.
A symbol of unity, a gleaming star,
Guiding us forward, near and far.

In fluorescence, you truly excel,
Your photons dance, a radiant spell.
From red to blue, a vivid glow,
Illuminating the darkness below.

In phosphors and lasers, you find your home,
Creating a kaleidoscope, a spectrum to roam.
Your vibrant hues, a celestial sight,
Captivating the world, both day and night.

Europium, a shining beacon of light,
A symbol of hope, burning bright.
May your luminescence never fade,
As we explore the universe you've made.

TWO

EUROPIUM, THE COSMIC POET

In a realm where atoms dance and collide,
Europium emerges with a mesmerizing stride.
A luminescent enigma, elusive and rare,
Unveiling secrets with an ethereal glare.

Within the realm of the periodic table's maze,
Europium enchants, its essence ablaze.
Symbolic of unity, a bridge it becomes,
Linking the elements, harmonizing as drums.

With sixty-three protons, it takes its place,
A beacon of brilliance, a celestial embrace.
Unveiling a spectrum, a vivid display,
Europium's radiance lights up the way.

In the dark corners of phosphorescent dreams,
Europium's luminescence softly beams.

A symphony of colors, a cosmic ballet,
It paints the universe in a celestial array.
    From deep crimson red to a sapphire blue,
Europium's magic stirs, enticing me and you.
In lasers it dances, a conductor of light,
Guiding us through the cosmos, pure and bright.
    So let us embrace this element of wonder,
Europium, the cosmic poet, the celestial ponder.
In its atomic dance, a story unfolds,
Of unity, luminescence, and mysteries untold.

THREE

SHINING BRIGHT

Europium, a celestial jewel, rare and distinct,
Within the periodic table, a treasure to be linked.
Atomic number sixty-three, you proudly reside,
In the realm of elements, your presence can't hide.

A symphony of electrons, dancing in your core,
In the cosmic orchestra, melodies they explore.
With an aura of mystery, you captivate the eye,
Europium, the enigmatic element, soaring high.

Your luminescent essence, a cosmic ballet,
In phosphorescent dreams, a vivid display.
From deep crimson to azure blue,
Your radiance paints the sky, a kaleidoscope true.

In the depths of the universe, you wander,
A celestial traveler, no boundaries to ponder.

With magnetic allure, you embrace the night,
Guiding lost souls towards the ethereal light.
 Europium, a symbol of unity and grace,
A testament to Europe's vibrant embrace.
Through science and art, your legacy thrives,
An inspiration to dreamers, where creativity survives.
 So let us celebrate your atomic glory,
Europium, the luminary of the cosmic story.
In your luminescence, we find hope and delight,
A radiant star, forever shining bright.

FOUR

YOUR RADIANCE

Europium, a celestial marvel, born of cosmic fire,
Within the vast expanse, your essence does inspire.
A luminescent gem, glowing with ethereal grace,
In the tapestry of elements, you find your place.

With atomic number sixty-three, you proudly stand,
A beacon of brilliance, crafted by nature's hand.
Your magnetic allure, like a celestial dance,
Attracts the curious minds, longing for a chance.

In the realm of phosphorescent dreams, you reign,
Your vibrant hues, an artist's brushstroke, untamed.
From crimson red to azure blue, a dazzling array,
Europium's radiance, a symphony on display.

Through the fabric of time and space, you traverse,
A traveler of dimensions, a cosmic universe.

Uniting the elements, a bridge you create,
In the depths of creation, your presence innate.
   Europium, a symbol of unity and bonds,
A luminary guiding us, where curiosity responds.
In the depths of laboratories, your secrets unfold,
Unraveling mysteries, stories yet untold.
   So let us cherish your luminescent glow,
Europium, an element that continues to show,
That even in the darkest nights, hope prevails,
With your radiance, the universe unveils.

FIVE

UNITY AND GRACE

Europium, an element rare and bright,
A cosmic jewel, a celestial light.
Within your atomic heart, mysteries reside,
A symphony of electrons, dancing with pride.
    In the tapestry of elements, you play your part,
A luminescent gem, a work of art.
From the depths of the Earth, you were brought forth,
To illuminate the world, from south to north.
    Your radiance, a palette of colors untold,
A painter's dream, a story yet unfold.
From crimson red to oceanic blue,
Europium, your luminescence, always true.
    In the realm of science, you hold the key,
Unlocking the secrets of the universe, for all to see.

Phosphors and lasers, your playground of creation,
Harnessing your power, a source of fascination.
    Europium, a symbol of unity and grace,
A beacon of light in the cosmic space.
Guiding us forward, like a celestial guide,
Through the vast expanse, where wonders reside.
    So let us celebrate your atomic glory,
Europium, the luminary of the cosmic story.
In your brilliance, we find inspiration and awe,
A testament to the beauty of natural law.

SIX

WONDERS OF THE NIGHT

Europium, element of rare allure,
Within your atomic heart, secrets pure.
A symphony of electrons, dancing in delight,
Illuminating the cosmos, a celestial light.

In the depths of phosphorescent dreams,
Europium's luminescence softly gleams.
Radiant hues, a vibrant display,
Casting a spell, enchanting the way.

From ruby red to sapphire blue,
Europium's brilliance shines through.
A kaleidoscope of colors, ever bright,
Guiding us through the darkest night.

Within its atomic embrace, unity resides,
Europium, a symbol of connection that abides.

An element of harmony, bridging the divide,
Uniting hearts and minds, side by side.
    So let us marvel at Europium's grace,
A cosmic dancer, a celestial embrace.
In its luminescent song, we find delight,
A testament to the wonders of the night.

SEVEN

SCIENCE DEFINES

Europium, a cosmic treasure, rare and divine,
Your luminescence, like stars that brightly shine.
With atomic beauty, you captivate our sight,
A beacon of brilliance, in the darkest of night.
 From the depths of creation, you gracefully emerge,
A symphony of colors, a celestial surge.
Crimson reds and azure blues, a painter's delight,
Europium, your radiance, a celestial light.
 In the realm of science, your secrets unfold,
Phosphorescent dreams, a story yet untold.
With magnetic allure, you dance in the air,
Guiding us towards knowledge, beyond compare.
 A symbol of unity, a bridge that connects,
Europium, the element that intersects.

In laboratories, your wonders are explored,
Unraveling mysteries, like never before.
 So let us embrace your atomic glow,
Europium, a marvel that continues to show,
That in the realm of elements, you truly shine,
A reminder of the wonders that science defines.

EIGHT

MAGIC THAT CHEMISTRY DERIVES

Europium, element of celestial hue,
In the realm of chemistry, a treasure so true.
With atomic number sixty-three,
Your luminescence captivates, setting hearts free.
    A symphony of colors, a cosmic dance,
Europium, your radiance enchants every glance.
From ruby red to cerulean blue,
You paint the universe, a mesmerizing view.
    In the depths of phosphorescent dreams,
Europium's glow, a celestial theme.
Guiding us through the cosmos, bright and clear,
Igniting curiosity, banishing fear.
    A symbol of unity, a bridge between worlds,
Europium, your presence unfurls.

From laboratories to distant stars,
You reveal the wonders, removing all bars.
    Let us celebrate your atomic glory,
Europium, the luminary of the cosmic story.
In your luminescence, we find hope and awe,
A testament to the beauty of natural law.
    So, shine on, Europium, forever bright,
A beacon of wonder, a guiding light.
In your element, the universe thrives,
A testament to the magic that chemistry derives.

NINE

EUROPIUM, A MARVEL

Europium, a celestial dancer, you shine so bright,
In the realm of elements, a captivating light.
From crimson red to cobalt blue,
Your luminescence dazzles, a mesmerizing hue.

In the depths of the cosmos, you gracefully roam,
A cosmic explorer, finding your own home.
With magnetic allure, you draw us near,
Revealing the mysteries we hold dear.

Europium, a symbol of unity and grace,
In laboratories, your secrets we embrace.
Phosphorescent dreams, you bring to life,
A symphony of colors, dispelling all strife.

Let us celebrate your atomic symphony,
Europium, a marvel for all to see.

In your radiance, beauty unfurls,
A testament to the wonders of the world.
　So, dance on, Europium, in the cosmic ballet,
Illuminate our minds, guide us on our way.
In your element, dreams come alive,
A reminder of the magic in which we thrive.

TEN

HARMONY AND GRACE

Europium, a luminary of cosmic hues,
A symphony of light, your brilliance accrues.
From crimson red to cerulean blue,
Your radiance captivates, enchanting the view.
In the tapestry of elements, you stand tall,
A beacon of unity, surpassing the thrall.
Phosphorescent dreams, you effortlessly weave,
Binding the universe, like a cosmic reprieve.
Amidst the laboratories, your secrets unfold,
Unveiling the wonders, a story yet untold.
Guiding us through the realms of knowledge,
Your luminescence shines, illuminating the edge.
Europium, a symbol of harmony and grace,
In your atomic embrace, unity takes place.

From distant galaxies to Earth's terrestrial abode,
Your presence ignites curiosity, a cosmic ode.
    Let us cherish your atomic artistry,
Europium, a marvel in the vast tapestry.
In your luminous dance, worlds collide,
A testament to the wonders, forever to reside.

ELEVEN

WONDERS OF CREATION

Europium, element of cosmic allure,
A radiant gem, shining pure.
In the realm of science, you hold the key,
Unveiling mysteries, for all to see.

Your luminescent hues, a celestial dance,
Casting a spell, captivating every glance.
From vivid reds to cool blues,
Your vibrant glow, forever infuse.

In laboratories, your secrets unfurl,
A beacon of knowledge, a captivating swirl.
Phosphorescent dreams, you bring to light,
Guiding us through the darkest night.

Europium, symbol of unity and grace,
A bridge between worlds, a cosmic embrace.

In your atomic realm, harmony resides,
Connecting the universe, like celestial tides.
   Let us celebrate your atomic might,
Europium, shining ever bright.
In your brilliance, we find inspiration,
A testament to the wonders of creation.

TWELVE

DAZZLING ELEMENT

Europium, oh radiant element of lore,
In your atomic embrace, mysteries galore.
Phosphorescent dreams, you vividly ignite,
A symphony of colors, a captivating sight.

From the laboratories to the vast expanse,
You traverse the cosmos in a cosmic dance.
With magnetic allure, you guide our way,
Unveiling the secrets of the night and day.

Europium, a symbol of unity profound,
Within your atomic structure, wonders are found.
A bridge between worlds, you gracefully unite,
Connecting hearts and minds, shining so bright.

Let us marvel at your luminescent glow,
Europium, a celestial light show.
In your radiance, curiosity takes flight,
Revealing the beauty of the scientific insight.

So, dance on, Europium, in cosmic harmony,
A dazzling element, forever to be.
As we explore the realms of the unknown,
You illuminate the path, a beacon brightly shown.

THIRTEEN

SCIENCE UNFOLD

Europium, a jewel in the cosmic sea,
Your luminescent glow, a captivating spree.
Within your atoms, a symphony resides,
A dance of electrons, where beauty abides.

In laboratories, your secrets unfold,
Unveiling the wonders, stories yet untold.
Phosphorescent dreams, you bring to life,
Igniting our imaginations, banishing strife.

Europium, a symbol of unity profound,
A bridge between worlds, where connections are found.
From distant galaxies to our earthly domain,
Your presence unites, erasing the mundane.

Let us celebrate your atomic grace,
Europium, a marvel in time and space.

In your radiance, colors intertwine,
Painting the universe with hues so fine.
    So, shine on, Europium, with celestial might,
A beacon of knowledge, guiding us through the night.
In your element, the wonders of science unfold,
A testament to the mysteries waiting to be told.

FOURTEEN

BEACON OF CURIOSITY

Europium, a jewel in the cosmic night,
A luminescent guardian, shining so bright.
In your atomic realm, mysteries reside,
A captivating element, impossible to hide.

Your radiance, a symphony of vibrant hues,
Phosphorescent dreams, sparking cosmic views.
From laboratories to the celestial sphere,
You captivate hearts, dispelling all fear.

Europium, a symbol of unity profound,
Connecting the universe, like a celestial sound.
With magnetic allure, you guide our way,
Revealing the wonders of night and day.

Let us celebrate your atomic splendor,
Europium, a cosmic marvel to remember.

In your luminescence, knowledge unfolds,
A testament to the stories chemistry holds.
   So, shine on, Europium, in celestial flight,
A beacon of curiosity, illuminating the night.
In your element, the universe thrives,
A symphony of atoms, where wonder survives.

FIFTEEN

EARTH'S EMBRACE

Europium, oh radiant star,
A luminescent jewel from afar.
In laboratories, your secrets reside,
Unveiling wonders with each stride.
   With a magnetic embrace, you draw us near,
Revealing mysteries, both far and near.
Phosphorescent dreams, you bring to life,
A symphony of colors, banishing strife.
   Europium, a symbol of unity's grace,
In your atomic realm, secrets we chase.
From deep within the Earth's embrace,
Your presence ignites, leaving no trace.
   Let us celebrate your atomic ballet,
Europium, guiding us on our way.

In your radiant glow, knowledge unfolds,
A testament to the stories chemistry holds.
    So dance on, Europium, with celestial might,
Illuminate our minds, shining so bright.
In your element, the universe thrives,
A cosmic symphony, where wonder survives.

SIXTEEN

NEVER ENDS

Europium, element of luminescent grace,
Your radiance paints the universe's space.
Within your atomic realm, secrets reside,
A cosmic symphony where wonders coincide.

Phosphorescent dreams, you bring to life,
A captivating dance, free from strife.
With vibrant hues, you light up the night,
Guiding our curiosity, like a cosmic light.

Europium, symbol of unity profound,
Connecting worlds, both lost and found.
From distant galaxies to our humble Earth,
You weave together the atoms of our birth.

Let us celebrate your atomic might,
Europium, shining ever bright.
In laboratories, your mysteries unfurl,
Unveiling the secrets of the scientific world.

So shine on, Europium, in celestial bliss,
A testament to the beauty of chemical abyss.
In your luminescent glow, knowledge ascends,
A beacon of inspiration that never ends.

SEVENTEEN

DAY BY DAY

In the realm of elements, you hold a special place,
Europium, with your luminescent grace.
A beacon of light, both rare and true,
Guiding our journey to discoveries anew.

Within your atomic structure, secrets reside,
Unveiling the universe, with each stride.
Phosphorescent dreams, you effortlessly weave,
Igniting the imagination, inspiring those who believe.

Europium, symbol of unity's embrace,
Connecting the cosmos, transcending space.
From stellar explosions to terrestrial ground,
Your presence unites, a cosmic sound.

Let us celebrate your atomic symphony,
Europium, a marvel for all to see.

In your vibrant glow, knowledge unfurls,
Revealing the wonders of this chemical world.
 So shine on, Europium, with brilliance untold,
A catalyst for innovation, forever bold.
In your luminescence, we find our way,
Exploring the mysteries, day by day.

EIGHTEEN

CELESTIAL GEM

Europium, a celestial gem,
Within your atomic embrace, wonders stem.
Phosphorescent dreams, you gracefully ignite,
Guiding the seekers with your radiant light.

In the depths of your atomic core,
A symphony of electrons forever soar.
With magnetic allure, you captivate,
Revealing the secrets that lie in wait.

Europium, a symbol of cosmic unity,
Connecting the realms with harmonious serenity.
From distant galaxies to our earthly abode,
You bridge the gaps, where knowledge is bestowed.

Let us celebrate your luminescent glow,
Europium, a beacon that continues to grow.
In your radiance, colors intertwine,
Painting the universe with hues divine.

So dance on, Europium, in stellar grace,
A catalyst of curiosity, leading the chase.
In your element, the mysteries unfurl,
A testament to the wonders of our physical world.

NINETEEN

TAPESTRY OF ATOMS

Europium, oh radiant star,
A luminescent beauty from afar.
Within your atomic heart, secrets reside,
Unveiling the cosmos, with every stride.
    Phosphorescent dreams, you bring to life,
A symphony of colors, erasing strife.
Your magnetic embrace pulls us near,
Guiding us through the celestial sphere.
    A symbol of unity, profound and vast,
Connecting the past, present, and future amassed.
From distant galaxies to earthly plains,
You illuminate the path where knowledge remains.
    Let us celebrate your atomic might,
Europium, shining with celestial light.

In laboratories, your mysteries unfold,
Revealing the tales that chemistry holds.
 So shine on, Europium, in cosmic embrace,
A luminary force, igniting our chase.
In your element, the universe thrives,
A tapestry of atoms, where wonder survives.

TWENTY

SPARKS THE SOUL

Europium, element of cosmic allure,
In your atomic dance, mysteries endure.
Phosphorescent dreams, shimmering bright,
Guiding us through the depths of the night.
    A symbol of unity, both rare and true,
Connecting the elements, old and new.
From ancient stardust to the Earth's embrace,
You grace the universe with your vibrant grace.
    Let us celebrate your luminescent glow,
Europium, a marvel that continues to grow.
In your spectral dance, knowledge unfurls,
Unveiling the wonders of the chemical world.
    So shine on, Europium, with brilliance and might,
A beacon of curiosity, forever alight.

In your elemental realm, we explore and learn,
Discovering the secrets that make the universe churn.
    With each atomic step, you lead the way,
Revealing the stories that atoms convey.
Europium, we cherish your unique role,
An element of wonder that sparks the soul.

TWENTY-ONE

ENLIGHTENS THE SOUL

Europium, a radiant jewel in the night,
A luminescent guide, shimmering bright.
In the depths of the periodic sea,
You beckon us with your atomic decree.

Symbol of unity, you bridge the divide,
Connecting the elements, side by side.
In your atomic core, mysteries reside,
Revealing the beauty of the chemical tide.

Let us celebrate your magnetic embrace,
Europium, a marvel in time and space.
Through your fluorescence, secrets unfold,
Unveiling the stories chemistry holds.

So shine on, Europium, with cosmic might,
A catalyst of knowledge, a celestial light.

In your luminescence, we find our way,
Exploring the wonders, day by day.
    With each electron's dance, you enchant,
A symphony of atoms, a cosmic chant.
Europium, we honor your unique role,
An element of wonder that enlightens the soul.

TWENTY-TWO

PRICELESS PEARL

Europium, gleaming essence afar,
A radiant star, a celestial memoir.
Within your atoms, secrets reside,
Unveiling the wonders, none can hide.
    In the depths of cosmic night,
You shimmer, casting a vibrant light.
A symphony of electrons, a dazzling display,
Guiding us through the darkness, leading the way.
    Symbol of unity, a bridge you create,
Connecting the elements, the fabric of fate.
From stellar explosions to terrestrial terrain,
You weave a tapestry, where knowledge remains.
    Let us celebrate your luminescent glow,
Europium, a beacon that continues to grow.

In your spectral dance, colors intertwine,
Painting the universe with hues divine.
 So shine on, Europium, in cosmic embrace,
A catalyst of curiosity, leaving no trace.
In your atomic realm, where wonders unfurl,
We find the beauty of science, a priceless pearl.

TWENTY-THREE

BRIDGING THE GAPS

Europium, element of cosmic allure,
A luminescent gem, so pure.
In the depths of the periodic table you reside,
With atomic number 63, your identity implied.

Your electrons dance in vibrant delight,
Illuminating the darkness, a celestial sight.
With a magnetic embrace, you captivate,
Unveiling the secrets that lie in wait.

Symbol of unity, bridging the gaps,
Connecting the realms, like intricate maps.
From stellar explosions to earthly realms,
You carry the knowledge, like ancient helms.

Let us celebrate your atomic symphony,
Europium, a marvel for all to see.
In your phosphorescent glow, dreams unfurl,

Guiding us through the mysteries of this chemical world.

So shine on, Europium, with brilliance untold,
A catalyst for innovation, forever bold.
In your luminescence, we find our way,
Exploring the cosmos, day by day.

TWENTY-FOUR

ELEMENT OF FASCINATION

Europium, a luminary in the night,
With atomic might, shining so bright.
In the vast expanse of the cosmic sea,
Your presence glimmers, a celestial decree.

Symbol of unity, bridging the divide,
Connecting the elements, side by side.
From distant galaxies to earthly terrain,
You weave the fabric of knowledge, without restrain.

Let us celebrate your magnetic allure,
Europium, a beacon, forever pure.
In your luminescent dance, colors unfold,
Revealing the secrets that chemistry holds.

So shine on, Europium, with cosmic grace,
A catalyst of discovery, leaving no trace.

In your atomic realm, the wonders ignite,
Unveiling the mysteries, like stars in flight.
　With each electron's symphony, you enchant,
A cosmic orchestra, harmonious and grand.
Europium, we marvel at your unique role,
An element of fascination that touches the soul.

TWENTY-FIVE

ELECTRON'S JOURNEY

Europium, element of luminescent delight,
With your atomic dance, you captivate the night.
A symphony of electrons, a celestial ballet,
You shimmer and glow, guiding our way.

Symbol of unity, bridging the gaps,
Connecting the elements, like intertwined straps.
From stellar explosions to earthly embrace,
You carry the secrets of time and space.

Let us celebrate your magnetic allure,
Europium, a treasure, forever pure.
In your phosphorescent embrace, stories unfold,
Revealing the wonders that chemistry holds.

So shine on, Europium, with brilliance untamed,
A catalyst for curiosity, never to be tamed.
In your atomic realm, the universe thrives,
Unveiling the mysteries that keep us alive.

With each electron's journey, you inspire,
Igniting our minds with passion and fire.
Europium, we marvel at your unique role,
An element of fascination that touches the soul.

TWENTY-SIX

UNIQUE ROLE

    Europium, oh radiant star,
In the realm of elements, you are,
With atomic grace and luminescent hue,
A wonder that captivates, through and through.
    Symbol of unity, a bridge you create,
Connecting the elements in a cosmic ballet.
From stellar explosions to terrestrial ground,
You weave a tapestry profound.
    Let us celebrate your vibrant glow,
Europium, a marvel, it's time to show,
In your spectral dance, colors unite,
Unraveling the mysteries, pure and bright.
    So shine on, Europium, with cosmic might,
A catalyst for knowledge, a celestial light.
In your atomic symphony, wisdom unfurls,
Guiding us through the secrets of the world.

With each electron's spin, you enchant,
A cosmic conductor, a magical chant.
Europium, we honor your unique role,
An element of wonder that touches the soul.

TWENTY-SEVEN

CATALYST OF DISCOVERY

Europium, a beacon shining bright,
A luminescent star in the night.
In your atomic embrace, secrets reside,
Revealing the wonders that chemistry hides.

Symbol of unity, you bridge the divide,
Connecting the elements, side by side.
From celestial skies to earthly terrain,
You carry the knowledge, a precious domain.

Let us celebrate your magnetic allure,
Europium, a gem that's ever pure.
In your phosphorescent glow, mysteries unfold,
Unveiling the stories that chemistry holds.

So shine on, Europium, with brilliance untamed,
A catalyst of discovery, forever unnamed.

In your atomic dance, colors intertwine,
Painting the universe with hues divine.
    With each electron's movement, you inspire,
Igniting the imagination, setting it on fire.
Europium, we marvel at your unique role,
An element of fascination that touches the soul.

TWENTY-EIGHT

WISDOM AND INSIGHT

Europium, a beacon of light,
Guiding us through the darkest night.
With atomic prowess, you mesmerize,
Unveiling secrets behind veiled skies.

Symbol of unity, you bridge the gaps,
Connecting worlds, like cosmic maps.
From stellar explosions to earthly embrace,
You hold the keys to the universe's grace.

Let us celebrate your luminescent glow,
Europium, a marvel that continues to grow.
In your spectral dance, colors intertwine,
Revealing the wonders of the chemical design.

So shine on, Europium, with brilliance untamed,
A catalyst for curiosity, forever unnamed.

In your atomic realm, knowledge thrives,
Unveiling the mysteries that keep us alive.
    With each electron's spin, you enchant,
A cosmic conductor, a celestial chant.
Europium, we honor your unique role,
An element of fascination that touches the soul.
    So let your light shine, oh Europium so bright,
Illuminate our path with wisdom and insight.
Through the depths of science, you lead the way,
Europium, forever in our hearts, you'll stay.

TWENTY-NINE

PERIODIC SCHEME

Europium, element of rare allure,
With your atomic presence, so pure.
A beacon of luminescence, shining bright,
Guiding us through the mysteries of the night.

In the depths of the periodic table you reside,
A treasure of discovery, impossible to hide.
From stellar explosions, you were born,
A cosmic gift, forever sworn.

Your magnetic charm, a cosmic thread,
Binding the elements, like words unsaid.
From the stars above to the Earth below,
You bring unity, a celestial flow.

Europium, conductor of atomic dance,
In your spectral symphony, we find a chance.
To explore the secrets that lie within,
Unveiling the wonders, where science begins.

So let your luminescence continue to gleam,
A symbol of knowledge, like a timeless dream.
Europium, we honor your unique role,
An element of fascination that touches the soul.
In the realm of chemistry, you reign supreme,
Europium, a jewel of the periodic scheme.
Forever cherished, forever adored,
Your presence in science, forever restored.

THIRTY

EUROPIUM, A JEWEL

Europium, oh radiant star,
You shimmer in the cosmos afar.
In the vast expanse of the universe's embrace,
You hold secrets woven in your atomic lace.
    With a magnetic allure, you captivate,
Bridging the elements, a cosmic mandate.
From celestial fires to earthly domain,
You bring harmony, an elemental chain.
    Europium, a luminescent guide,
In your vibrant glow, knowledge resides.
Phosphorescent whispers, colors unfold,
Revealing the wonders that chemistry holds.
    So shine on, Europium, with brilliance untamed,
A catalyst for discovery, forever unnamed.

In your atomic dance, mysteries unfurl,
Unlocking the secrets of our intricate world.
    With each electron's rhythm, you inspire,
Igniting curiosity, fueling the fire.
Europium, we honor your unique role,
An element of fascination, enriching the soul.
    In the tapestry of elements, you stand,
Europium, a jewel, crafted by cosmic hand.
Forever celebrated, forever adored,
Your presence in science, forever restored.

THIRTY-ONE

EUROPIUM SO RARE

Oh, Europium, a beacon of light,
In the realm of chemistry, shining so bright.
With your atomic charm and magnetic grace,
You bring unity to the cosmic space.

From stellar explosions to Earth's embrace,
You hold the secrets, a celestial trace.
Phosphorescent hues, a mesmerizing dance,
Revealing the mysteries, captivating chance.

So radiate, Europium, with brilliance divine,
A catalyst for knowledge, a treasure to find.
In your atomic realm, discoveries ignite,
Unveiling the wonders that science excites.

With each electron's spin, you inspire,
Igniting curiosity, fueling the fire.
Europium, we honor your unique role,
An element of fascination that touches the soul.

In the tapestry of elements, you stand,
Europium, a luminescent strand.
Forever celebrated, forever adored,
Your presence in science, forever restored.
So let your light shine, oh Europium so rare,
Guiding us through the mysteries we dare.
In the realm of chemistry, you'll forever remain,
Europium, a symbol of knowledge we sustain.

THIRTY-TWO

SPARK THE FLAME

Europium, a beacon of cosmic grace,
In the universe's fabric, you find your place.
With a luminescent radiance, you shine so bright,
Guiding us through the depths of scientific insight.

In your atomic dance, colors intertwine,
Revealing the secrets of the chemical design.
A catalyst for curiosity, you spark the flame,
Igniting a passion for knowledge we can't tame.

Oh Europium, element of allure,
Your presence in science is forever pure.
From stellar explosions to terrestrial land,
You hold the key to understanding, hand in hand.

With each electron's spin, a symphony unfolds,
Unraveling the mysteries that nature beholds.
Europium, we honor your unique role,
A treasure of the periodic table, captivating the soul.

So let your brilliance shine, oh radiant star,
Leading us closer to answers, near and far.
Europium, a symbol of wisdom and light,
In the realm of elements, you shine ever bright.

THIRTY-THREE

EXPANSE OF SCIENCE

Europium, the luminescent gem,
A symbol of curiosity, a precious diadem.
In your atomic dance, colors come alive,
Revealing the secrets that within you thrive.
    Oh Europium, conductor of light,
Guiding us through the mysteries of the night.
With each electron's spin, a symphony unfolds,
Unveiling the wonders that chemistry holds.
    In the cosmic tapestry, you have your place,
A celestial messenger, a cosmic embrace.
Europium, we honor your unique role,
An element of fascination that awakens the soul.
    From stellar explosions to earthly abode,
You navigate the realms, a celestial ode.

With each pulse of energy, you ignite,
The spark of knowledge, burning ever bright.
    So shine on, Europium, with brilliance untamed,
A beacon of discovery, forever unnamed.
In the vast expanse of science, you are our guide,
Europium, forever in our hearts, you reside.

THIRTY-FOUR

UNIVERSE'S DECREE

    Europium, a luminescent jewel in the night,
A celestial dancer, a captivating sight.
In your atomic embrace, mysteries unfold,
Revealing a tale that's waiting to be told.
    With each electron's twirl, a cosmic ballet,
You paint the universe in a vibrant display.
Europium, we honor your unique role,
An element of wonder, igniting the soul.
    From stellar birth to Earth's fertile ground,
You grace us with beauty, profound and profound.
A catalyst for knowledge, a guide through the unknown,
Europium, your brilliance forever shown.
    In the depths of science, you hold the key,
Unlocking the secrets of the universe's decree.

With each spectral fingerprint, a story is told,
Of the elements' dance, forever bold.
  So shine on, Europium, with radiant grace,
Illuminate our minds in this vast cosmic space.
Europium, forever cherished, forever adored,
A luminary element, forever restored.

THIRTY-FIVE

FOREVER CHERISHED

Europium, element of celestial light,
In your atomic realm, mysteries take flight.
A luminescent dance, a symphony of electrons,
Revealing the secrets that science beckons.

Like a star in the night, you shimmer and gleam,
Guiding us through the realm of the unseen.
With each spectral line, an enchanting tale,
Unveiling the wonders that atoms entail.

Oh Europium, a beacon of knowledge profound,
Your presence in science, forever renowned.
A catalyst for discovery, a guide through the dark,
Igniting the flame of curiosity's spark.

In the tapestry of elements, you hold a unique place,
A luminary jewel, interstellar grace.

Europium, we honor your radiant hue,
A symbol of wisdom, forever true.
　　So let your luminescence forever shine,
Inspiring minds with discoveries divine.
Europium, a testament to the wonders of creation,
Forever cherished, in science's celebration.

ABOUT THE AUTHOR

Walter the Educator is one of the pseudonyms for Walter Anderson. Formally educated in Chemistry, Business, and Education, he is an educator, an author, a diverse entrepreneur, and he is the son of a disabled war veteran. "Walter the Educator" shares his time between educating and creating. He holds interests and owns several creative projects that entertain, enlighten, enhance, and educate, hoping to inspire and motivate you.

Follow, find new works, and stay up to date
with Walter the Educator™
at WaltertheEducator.com

www.ingramcontent.com/pod-product-compliance
Lightning Source LLC
LaVergne TN
LVHW051959060526
838201LV00059B/3732